Stars and Planets

Carole Stott

KINGFISHER

NEW YORK

KINGFISHER
LONDON & NEW YORK

Copyright © Kingfisher 2011
Published in the United States by Kingfisher,
175 Fifth Ave., New York, NY 10010
Kingfisher is an imprint of Macmillan Children's Books, London.
All rights reserved.

Distributed in the U.S. by Macmillan, 175 Fifth Ave.,
New York, NY 10010
Distributed in Canada by H.B. Fenn and Company Ltd.,
34 Nixon Road, Bolton, Ontario L7E 1W2

Library of Congress Cataloging-in-Publication data
has been applied for.

Illustrations by Peter Bull Art Studio

ISBN 978-0-7534-6498-4

Kingfisher books are available for special promotions and premiums.
For details contact: Special Markets Department, Macmillan,
175 Fifth Avenue, New York, NY 10010.

For more information, please visit www.kingfisherbooks.com

Printed in China
1 3 5 7 9 8 6 4 2
1TR/1210/WKT/UNTD/140MA

FOR RUBY, MARTHA, AND ELIZA

Picture credits

**The Publisher would like to thank the following
for permission to reproduce their material
(t = top, b = bottom, c = center, l = left, r = right):**
Page 4tl & 4cr Hubble/NASA/STSci; 4bl Shutterstock/Plutonius
3d; 5cl NASA/University of Arizona; 5br Photolibrary/The Travel
Library; 6tl Science Photo Library (SPL)/Jerry Schad; 8cl SPL/G.
Bacon/European Space Agency (ESA)/NASA/STSci; 8bl SPL/
Larry Landolfi; 8br Hubble/NASA/STSci; 9tl & 9tr Hubble/NASA/
STSci; 9b European Space Observatory; 10bl NASA; 12l & 12br
NASA/Apollo Program; 12cr Photolibary/Comstock; 13t & 13bl
NASA/Apollo Program; 13r SPL/Eckhard Slawik; 14tl European
Space Observatory; 16l NASA/Hinode; 16tc NASA/German
Aerospace Center/DLR; 16br ESO/Philippe Federici; 17tr NASA/
Hubble; 17cl NASA/U.S. Geological Survey; 17bl SPL/Mark
Garlick; 17br SPL/Mark Garlick; 18bl NASA/JPL; 20bl SPL/
Francis Menage/Starsem; 20cr SPL/NASA; 21t SPL/NASA;
21bl SPL/Ria Novosti; 21tr & 21br ESA; 22b SPL/Detlev van
Ravenswaay; 24l, 24r, & 25t ISS/NASA; 25tr, 25cl, & 25cr SPL/
NASA; 25bl & 25br NASA; 26tl ESA; 28cl NASA/JPL; 28bl
NASA/Cornell University; 28tr SPL/David Ducros; 29cl NASA/
JPL; 29tr ESA; 29bc NASA/Goddard Space Flight Center; 29br
NASA/JPL; 30tl SPL/Tony & Daphne Hallas; 30cl Photolibrary/
Peter Arnold; 30cr & 30br ESA; 31tr, 31c, & 31bc ISS/NASA;
31cl Shutterstock/Vasily Smimov; 31bl SPL/Ria Novosti

Contents

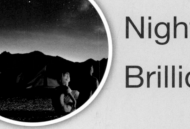

More to explore

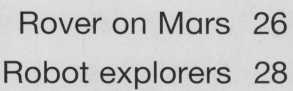

On some of the pages in this book, you will find colored buttons with symbols on them. There are four different colors, and each belongs to a different topic. Choose a topic, follow its colored buttons through the book, and you'll make some interesting discoveries of your own.

For example, on page 7 you'll find a blue button, like this, near the people looking at the sky. The blue buttons are about people discovering space.

Page 19

Human exploration

There is a page number in the button. Turn to that page (page 19) to find a blue button next to another example of human exploration. Follow the steps through the book, and at the end of your journey you'll discover how the steps are linked and even more information about this topic.

Technology

Discovery

Science

The other topics in this book are technology, discovery, and science. Follow the steps and see what you can discover!

All about space

Earth is our home in space. The Sun, the Moon, the stars, and everything else beyond Earth are all in space. All of these things together make the universe. The universe was born more than 13 billion years ago.

Mars

Mars's surface is covered in red soil.

Jupiter

Eight planets are in the part of space close to the Sun. Four of them are smaller planets made of rock and metal. They include Earth and Mars. Jupiter is one of the other four planets, which are much bigger and made mostly of gas.

Stars are huge spinning balls of hot, glowing gas. There are billions of them in space. The closest star to Earth is the Sun. The rest are so far away that they look like pinpoints of sparkling light.

From space, you can see Earth's land, oceans, and clouds.

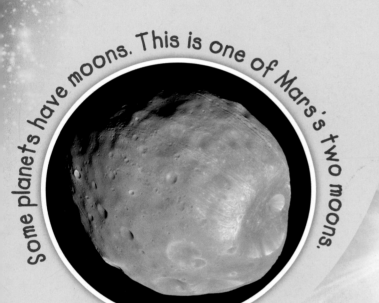

Some planets have moons. This is one of Mars's two moons.

Earth's surface is about one-fourth land, and the rest is water. Earth is the only place in space where we know life exists.

The Sun gives Earth light and warmth.

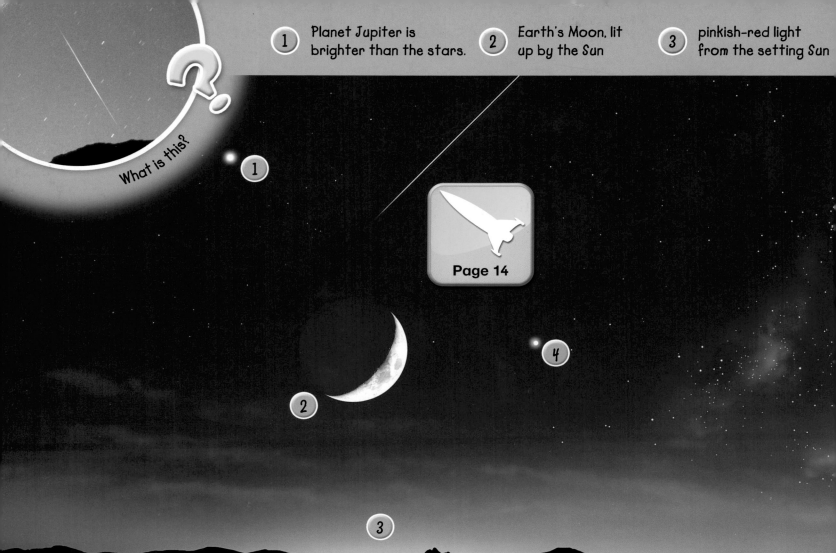

Page 14

1 Planet Jupiter is brighter than the stars.

2 Earth's Moon, lit up by the Sun

3 pinkish-red light from the setting Sun

What is this?

Nighttime stars

Earth's sky is full of stars and other things in space. We can see them once the Sun has set and the sky has gotten dark. Some stars are brighter than others. Venus, Jupiter, and other distant planets can look like bright stars, too.

Campers gaze up at the sky on a cloudless night. They can see the Moon, two planets, and countless stars. All of the stars that are visible at night—and our daytime Sun, too—belong to a huge collection of stars known as a galaxy. Our galaxy is called the Milky Way because its stars make a milky path of light across the sky.

Page 19

This is a meteor—a streak of light made by space dust shooting through Earth's atmosphere.

Brilliant stars

Stars in the night sky might look the same, but each one is unique. Stars are different sizes, colors, and temperatures, and some shine brighter than others. Stars don't last forever. They are born, change as they age, and eventually die.

Sirius

This white dwarf star lives near Sirius in space.

Sirius is the brightest star in the night sky. This huge white star is twice as big as the Sun and 25 times brighter.

The Cat's Eye Nebula is a star near the end of its life. It has pushed away its outer layers of gas, and these have made colorful, cloudy shells. They surround what's left of the central star.

Cat's Eye Nebula, a dying star

Constellations are imaginary patterns in the night sky made by connecting the brightest stars. This constellation is called Cygnus (the Swan).

center of the
Milky Way

star
cluster

The young stars in this star
cluster are very hot and glow
blue. They are surrounded
by gas and dust that will
make more stars.

Arms of stars spiral
out from the center
of the galaxy.

This red supergiant star is near the end of its life. It is called Betelgeuse.

The Milky Way galaxy
is round and flat and
shaped a little like a CD.
It is made of about 400
billion stars, as well as
a lot of gas and dust.

Betelgeuse is
pushing away gas
into space.

Space neighbor

The closest object to Earth in space is the Moon. It is a huge ball of rock that travels around our planet. It appears as the biggest, brightest thing in the night sky. The Moon doesn't have any light of its own, though—it shines brightly because sunlight bounces off its surface.

What is this?

Page 27

1 model of a spacecraft that landed on the Moon

2 photo of the Moon partly lit by sunshine

3 binoculars for viewing the Moon

This is a map of the Moon's surface. It shows the sites of different Moon landings.

11

Page 30

Page 26

6

A young girl gazes out her window at the Moon. Tonight it is full, which means that she can see the whole disk. She has just recorded its shape in her notebook. She can see the Moon's highlands and lowlands as brighter and darker areas. Binoculars or a telescope provide a close-up view of the Moon's dry surface, which is covered in craters.

4 drawings of the Moon made at different dates

5 poster showing the Moon's path around Earth

 6 A telescope shows the Moon close up.

On the Moon

The Moon has been studied a lot because it is so close to Earth. Thanks to telescopes and robot explorers, we have photos and maps of its entire surface. Astronauts have also visited the Moon and brought back some of its rocks.

viewing the Moon

Inside this space suit is Buzz Aldrin, the second person to walk on the Moon.

An astronaut is someone who travels into space. Twenty-four astronauts have flown as far as the Moon, and 12 of them landed on its surface.

A telescope shows mountains, flat plains, and thousands of small craters on the surface of the Moon.

Astronauts left footprints in the Moon's fine-grained soil.

Buzz Aldrin's footprint

new moon—its face is unlit

waxing crescent

first quarter

waxing gibbous

full moon—its face is fully lit

waning gibbous

last quarter

waning crescent

A lunar rover is an electric car built for driving across the Moon. Three spacecraft took rovers and astronauts to the Moon. The men returned to Earth, but the three rovers are still there.

This rover carried astronauts and the Moon rocks that they collected.

There are round craters all over the Moon's surface.

Space rocks made craters when they crashed into the Moon billions of years ago.

The Moon takes about a month to travel around Earth. As it moves, different parts of it are lit by the Sun. This makes it look as if the Moon is changing shape. The different shapes are called phases. Some have special names.

Page 27

| 1 | Sun | 2 | Mercury | 3 | Venus |
| 7 | Jupiter | 8 | Saturn | 9 | Uranus |

What is this?

Nearby space

Our Earth and Moon are part of the solar system—
a family of space objects that travel around the Sun.
The Sun is the biggest object in the solar system. Next
in size are the eight planets. There are also billions of small
bodies such as dwarf planets, moons, asteroids, and comets.

This is what we would see if we could travel away from Earth and beyond the solar system planets. It also shows the planets' paths, or orbits, around the Sun. The rock and metal planets—Mercury, Venus, Earth, and Mars—are closest to the Sun. Farther out is the largest planet, Jupiter, then Saturn, Uranus, and Neptune. These four all have rings. Far beyond, in distant space, are the stars of the Miiky Way.

Page 30

This is an asteroid—a lump of rock in the asteroid belt between Mars and Jupiter.

Different worlds

When we look closely at the solar system objects, we can see that they are very different worlds. They differ in size, what they are made of, and what their surfaces are like. The objects closest to the Sun are hottest. Things get colder and darker farther away from the Sun.

Callisto

Ganymede

Europa

Io

Jupiter has the most moons—more than 60! The largest four are Ganymede, Callisto, Io, and Europa. Ganymede is the biggest moon in the solar system.

The Sun is made of hot gas all the way through it, and it does not have a solid surface. Jets of gas burst out of it all the time.

jets of gas bigger than Earth

When Comet Hale-Bopp moved close to the Sun, it grew two tails.

white dust tail
and blue gas tail

Saturn

There are billions of asteroids in the asteroid belt.

...This asteroid is called Gaspra.

The picture below shows the **dwarf planet Pluto** in the sky of one of its moons, Charon. The two objects are both icy worlds about 40 times farther from the Sun than Earth is.

icy, rocky Pluto

Saturn is a pale yellow color but looks different here. The camera that took this picture used a type of light called ultraviolet light. It makes the different gases in Saturn's surface appear as different-colored bands.

Uranus has rings that seem to go around it from top to bottom. They are actually around the planet's middle, but Uranus is not upright. It was knocked over billions of years ago and spins on its side.

Uranus

Going into space

Anything going into space is taken there by a rocket. The journey starts on a launch pad, where the rocket waits to lift off the ground. Onboard is its cargo—a spacecraft heading for a planet or a craft with astronauts inside.

Two astronauts and their spacecraft are in the nose end of a rocket waiting to blast off. The rocket's supporting framework is lowering away. Another rocket is just lifting off. Once it is in the air, its first part, or stage, falls away. Its second stage continues into space, where it releases the spacecraft to travel onward on its own.

Page 15

What is this?

1 robotic spacecraft inside rocket

2 The first stage lifts the rocket off the ground.

3 control center, where a team manages the launch

This is a radio dish. It picks up radio signals from spacecraft in space so that they can be tracked.

19

4

Page 23

Page 23

5

6

4   astronauts inside their spacecraft

5   rocket on launch pad

6   fuel inside the rocket

Space journey

A rocket's job is to get a spacecraft into space. It takes months to build, but its work is done in a few minutes. The spacecraft's mission can last days or years. Robotic spacecraft, which have no astronauts onboard, can stay in space forever.

A rocket is used only once. A new one is built for each space journey. When it is ready, it is moved to its launch pad, where its tanks are filled with fuel.

Soyuz rocket

Flight controllers are people who watch over a spacecraft once it has been launched. They follow its journey day and night until the craft finishes its mission.

The Soyuz rocket is put together lying down and then raised upright for its launch.

Soyuz-FG

Hot gas comes out of the rocket's first stage and four booster rockets.

Green dye released into the ocean makes the spacecraft easy to spot.

Astronauts returning to Earth usually land in their home country, but these two came down in the ocean. A waiting ship took them back to the shore.

Ariane 5

booster rocket

The first person in space was Yuri Gagarin in 1961.

Gagarin was in space for 108 minutes.

Rockets come in different sizes depending on their cargo. The Ariane 5 is one of the biggest—as tall as a 15-story building. It can carry three spacecraft at once. The Soyuz-FG carries people and is smaller and slimmer.

Space walk

Astronauts go outside their spacecraft for all sorts of reasons—to build space stations, repair broken spacecraft, or carry out experiments. During a space walk, astronauts wear space suits that protect them and supply them with oxygen gas to breathe.

Two astronauts are space-walking outside the International Space Station—a huge spacecraft that travels around Earth 15 times each day. They have been attaching a new part to the station. Their tools are specially designed for their gloved hands. They are connected to tool belts so that they don't float away into space.

①

Page 30

What is this?

① Earth below has blue oceans and white clouds.

 Parts of the station are called modules.

 The space suit protects the astronaut's body.

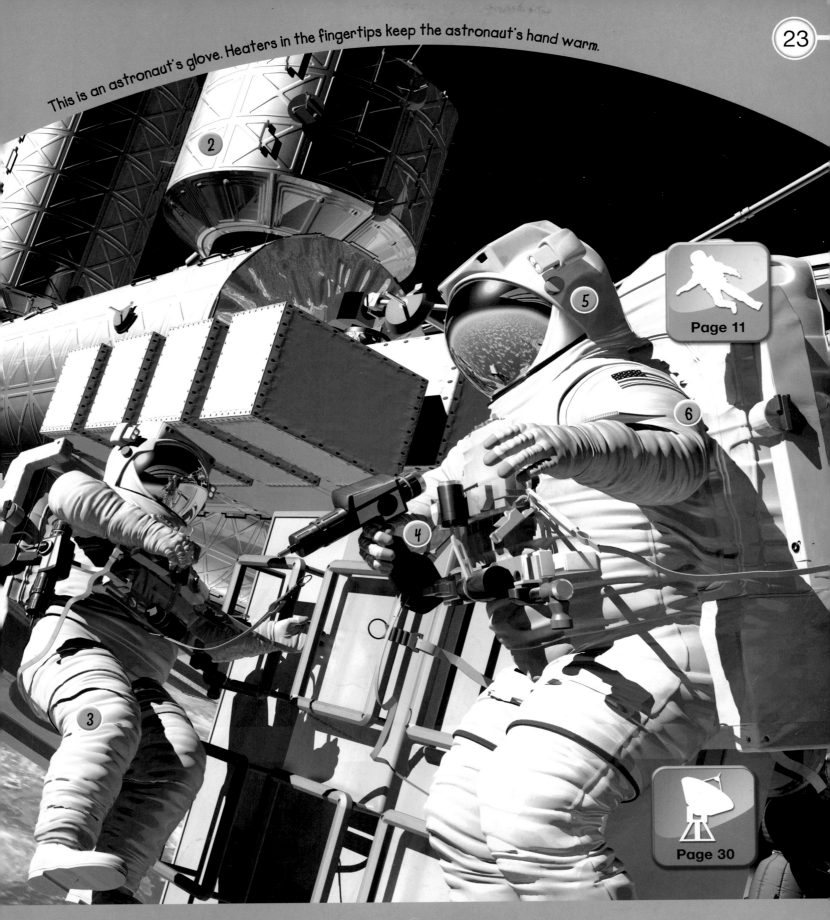

This is an astronaut's glove. Heaters in the fingertips keep the astronaut's hand warm.

Page 11

Page 30

 The hand drill is powered by batteries.

5 The helmet contains a telephone system so the astronauts can talk to each other.

 A checklist worn on the sleeve lists the jobs to do.

Living in space

Astronauts are living in space right now on the International Space Station. They work, relax, and eat just as we do on Earth. But one big difference is that astronauts feel weightless and float around.

Sleeping bags are attached to the space station's walls so sleeping astronauts don't move around. The astronauts have eight hours of rest and are woken by a different piece of music each day.

The astronaut's arms are weightless and move around as he sleeps.

A harness stops the astronaut from floating away.

Astronauts exercise for at least two hours each day. Their bodies don't have to work as hard in weightless space, so their muscles weaken if they don't get plenty of exercise.

astronaut on a treadmill

Extravehicular activity, or EVA, is the correct name for a space walk. Only those astronauts going on EVA wear space suits.

new part to attach to the space station

The International Space Station is a space home and workplace. It was launched in parts and then joined together by space-walking astronauts. It is about the size of a soccer field.

Solar panels make electricity for the space station.

space food

Some space foods are ready to eat; others need to have water added or be heated. Astronauts consume three meals a day, as well as snacks and drinks.

This astronaut is ready to go on EVA.

Under the space suit, the astronaut wears a special undergarment. It contains tubes of water to keep his body cool.

Fresh fruit is brought by astronauts arriving at the station.

Tubes contain cooled water.

checklist of EVA work

Page 19

What is this?

1 Opportunity arrives, covered in air bags.

2 The casing opens on top of the deflated air bags.

3 pink Martian sky

Rover on Mars

Spacecraft have traveled to all the solar system planets. The craft look down and take photographs as they fly past these distant worlds or as they travel around them. Some land and investigate. A few of these, called rovers, drive across their surfaces.

Opportunity has been exploring Mars ever since it arrived in 2004. Inflated air bags protected the rover as it landed. After bouncing and rolling, it stopped and the air bags deflated. Then its casing opened, and the rover drove off. *Opportunity* moves slowly across Mars. Every few feet it stops to study its surroundings.

Page 22

Page 18

⑥

④

⑤

This is Mars Express, a spacecraft that takes photos of Mars as it travels around it.

Robot explorers

Some spacecraft explore distant worlds that are too dangerous or too far away for astronauts to visit. Onboard computers tell these robot explorers what to do. The craft also receive extra instructions sent by radio from Earth.

Signals from the dish take 90 minutes to reach Earth.

Voyager 1 is the farthest spacecraft from Earth. It was launched in 1977 and flew past Jupiter in 1979 and Saturn in 1980. Now it is heading out of the solar system.

Cassini is traveling around Saturn and some of its moons. It gave a ride to a smaller craft called *Huygens*, which it released to parachute down to the surface of Saturn's largest moon, Titan.

Cameras are the robot's eyes.

photo of Beagle Crater on Mars by Opportunity

Opportunity

Opportunity and its twin, *Spirit* (also on Mars), have taken pictures of the planet's surface. They show us what we would see if we could walk on Mars.

Cassini

Rosetta is on its way to a comet. It will arrive in 2014 after a ten-year trip from Earth. Then it will journey with the comet as it travels around the Sun.

Rosetta *passed by* the asteroid Steins as it traveled through the asteroid belt.

Jupiter

Jupiter's moon Io

New Horizons has flown by Jupiter and is on target to arrive at the dwarf planet Pluto in 2015. As it flies by, its seven instruments will find out what Pluto is made of and how cold it is, and map its surface.

An electric generator provides power.

photo of Africa by Landsat

Satellites are spacecraft that travel around Earth. Some photograph our planet from space. They study its land, oceans, ice, and atmosphere. The Landsat satellites have been watching over Earth for 40 years.

Landsat

Looking into the night sky is a great way to discover things in space. You may be lucky enough to spot a **meteor** (shooting star)—or even a whole shower of them.

Comets are huge, dirty "snowballs" that exist far out in space, beyond the planets. Occasionally, a comet travels close to the Sun. Then it is big enough and bright enough to be seen in Earth's sky.

Discovery

notebook

By recording **observations**, scientists notice patterns and can predict events. That is how people discovered that the lunar phases are repeated every 29.5 days. *Lunar* means "having to do with the Moon."

Solar means "having to do with the Sun." The **solar panels** on the Martian rover turn sunlight into electricity. This is stored in batteries and used to power the craft and its equipment.

Science

People who study the stars and planets are called **astronomers**. The first ones used only their eyes to view the night sky. Today, telescopes and spacecraft help astronomers see more than ever.

telescopes, Hawaii

Just over 500 **astronauts** have been into space. They are mostly men but include more than 50 women. They have come from about 40 different countries.

rocket carrying crew to the ISS

Human exploration

Technology

A telescope collects light from an object in space and uses it to produce a magnified image. This helpful tool lets us see things more clearly and in greater detail.

Orbiters such as *Mars Express* are spacecraft that travel around planets or other objects in the solar system. Orbiters work for a few years, mapping the whole surface of a planet and testing its atmosphere.

Mars Express

More to explore

Cameras on spacecraft show us things that we cannot see from Earth. Images are recorded on a craft's computer and then sent to Earth as radio signals.

cameras on *Opportunity* rover

Onboard the **International Space Station** (ISS), astronauts are finding out what it is like to live in space for months at a time. Their experience will help plan for future trips to the planet Mars.

ISS

A rocket is powered by engines that burn fuel and produce hot gas. This gas pushes out of the bottom end of the rocket at high speed. The rocket is forced upward in the opposite direction of the gas.

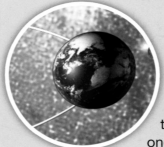

A force called gravity keeps all the planets on their paths, or **orbits**, around the Sun. Earth takes a year to make one complete path.

Space walks usually last several hours, and the astronauts are kept busy the whole time. Astronauts have spent a total of about 800 hours space-walking outside the ISS.

space-walking astronaut

The Moon is the only world besides Earth that humans have visited. Twelve people have walked on its surface. The first manned mission to land was in 1969, and the last was in 1972.

the Moon

Rockets have been going into space for 60 years. They lift off from about 30 launch sites around the world. Only three countries have built rockets to launch astronauts—the U.S., Russia, and China.

Space suits give astronauts their own Earthlike environment. They are made of many layers of material that hold in oxygen and keep astronauts at a constant temperature.

Index